SOUTHERN COOKING

Beryl Frank

WEATHERVANE
BOOKS

Thanks to the noble editor and the equally noble husband, both of whom always say—you can do it.

contents

introduction

The problem with a Southern cookbook is the extreme variety of Southern cooking. The range goes from elegantly served dishes from the Colonial Williamsburg era to simple home fare such as dandelion greens. The problem? It all tastes so very good.

In compiling this cookbook, no attempt was made to include everything a Southern cook makes. Hopefully, you will find some new ideas to try in your own kitchen, whether that kitchen is in Alaska or Alabama. If you like what you find here, you will go on to try other Southern specialties that are not included. The Southern cook is a very special person. Hopefully, this book will do you justice and you will discover new taste delights for your family.

a word about the recipes

Throughout this book the term "butter" has been used liberally. There are very few recipes, if any, where cholesterol-free margarine cannot be substituted for butter.

This is a modern cookbook, and shortcuts for time have been included. No plantation cook of the nineteenth century had such conveniences as canned cream of celery soup or frozen fish. Since we live in the twentieth century, we can take advantage of these fast foods and be thankful we have them. Many are included to make your cooking more enjoyable and still tasty.

Finally, don't be afraid to make a change for your personal family taste in any recipe here. The creative cook will add a dash of dillweed here or some okra there, as the mood suits. This is how new recipes are born. The ladies of the South cooked as the mood pleased them and food was available. Do the same when you cook—and you and your family will truly have happy eating.

appetizers

cheese fritters

1 egg, beaten
½ cup milk
1 teaspoon Worcestershire sauce
1 small onion, minced fine
Dash of hot pepper (optional)

2 cups biscuit mix
1½ cups diced American
   cheese
Fat for deep frying
Jelly or jam of your choice

Mix egg, milk, Worcestershire sauce, onion, pepper, and prepared biscuit mix in a bowl. Blend well; stir in cheese.

Preheat fat in skillet. Drop mixture by teaspoonfuls into hot fat. Fry until golden-brown fritters. Drain on paper towels.

Serve fritters next to a dish of your favorite jelly or jam for dipping. Makes about 40 fritters.

ham and melon balls

6 to 8 ounces ham, sliced very thin
Honeydew melon, cantaloupe, or Spanish melon

Slice ham into pieces 1 inch wide by 4 inches long. These will wrap comfortably around melon balls.

Cut melon into balls; place on paper towels to drain excess water. Wrap each melon ball with ham; secure with toothpick. Refrigerate until ready to serve. Makes 24 to 36 balls.

shrimp party crepes

1 pound fresh shrimp, boiled, cleaned, deveined
1 tablespoon lemon juice
3 tablespoons freshly grated Parmesan cheese
1 tablespoon chopped chives
2 tablespoons mayonnaise
3 tablespoons sour cream
$\frac{1}{8}$ teaspoon salt
White pepper to taste
1 recipe your favorite crepes, cooked, stacked, ready
Melted butter

Combine shrimp, lemon juice, cheese, chives, mayonnaise, sour cream, salt, and pepper in mixing bowl; mix until well-blended.

Place crepes, 6 to 7 inches round, on baking dish. Spoon shrimp filling into each crepe; fold over crepe. Brush with melted butter. Heat under broiler or in hot oven several minutes, until lightly browned.

Remove crepes to serving dish; serve at once. Makes about 16 crepes.

shrimp party crepes

sweet-potato fingers

sweet-potato fingers

Keep these tasty appetizers on a hot tray until party time. They'll go fast.

4 to 6 cooked sweet potatoes
$\frac{1}{4}$ cup flour
Fat for deep frying
$\frac{1}{2}$ cup brown sugar
1 teaspoon salt
$\frac{1}{2}$ teaspoon nutmeg

Cut sweet potatoes into strips or fingers. Score lightly with fork. Dip each finger into flour until well-coated.

Heat fat in medium skillet. Fry potato fingers until golden brown. Drain on paper towels. Sprinkle with mixture of brown sugar, salt, and nutmeg. Makes about 40 fingers.

sausage biscuits

This is an easy appetizer that can be prepared weeks ahead, frozen, and put into the oven when ready to serve.

8 ounces sharp cheddar cheese, grated

1 pound hot pork sausage
2 cups biscuit mix

Mix everything together in bowl, working in sausage and cheese well. Drop onto ungreased cookie sheets; shape slightly with your fingers if you wish. Bake at 400°F about 15 minutes or until nicely browned.

Serve biscuits piping hot. Makes about 3 dozen biscuits.

sausage pies

1 recipe pie crust
¾ pound sausage

20 to 24 cherry tomatoes, halved

Prepare pie crust in your usual way; set aside.

Break up sausage in heavy skillet; cook until all pink has disappeared, about 10 minutes. Drain off fat on paper towels.

Roll out pie-crust dough; cut into 4-inch squares. Moisten corner of each square with a little cold water. Place squares on lightly greased baking sheet. Spoon drained sausage, about 1 spoonful per square, into center of each square. Pinch corners to seal, but don't close completely. Bake at 450°F 12 to 15 minutes. Then place half of cherry tomato, cut-side-down, on top of sausage—this is why you didn't seal the pie crust. Bake 10 minutes more or until pie crust is golden brown. Serve at once. Makes 20 to 24 pies.

spinach and crab supreme

1 bunch green onions and tops, minced
1 clove garlic, crushed
¼ pound butter
1 tablespoon Parmesan cheese
Salt, pepper, and Tabasco to taste

1 pound flaked crab meat
2 packages frozen chopped spinach, cooked as directed, drained

Sauté onions and garlic in butter in small skillet. Add this plus remaining ingredients to cooked spinach, stirring gently to mix well. Add extra seasonings if needed.

Put this into chafing dish to warm. Serve with your favorite cocktail cracker. Makes 1 ample chafing dish.

open peanut-butter sandwiches

16 pieces bread, crusts removed, quartered or cut into triangles
1½ cups peanut butter
¼ pound butter

1 cup shredded carrots
1½ cups finely chopped celery
2 teaspoons salt
Stuffed green olives for garnish

Set bread aside, saving crusts for some future bread stuffing.

Mix rest of ingredients except olives to form smooth spread; spread onto each piece of bread.

Top with stuffed green olive for color; arrange on serving plate. Makes about 60 sandwiches.

shrimp balls

1 medium onion, grated
1 medium raw potato, grated
1½ pounds raw shrimp, shelled,
   deveined, grated

1 egg
Salt and pepper to taste
Fat for deep frying

Grind or grate onion, potato, and shrimp into large bowl. Stir in egg, salt, and pepper. Potato is the thickening; batter will be thick.
Heat deep fat; drop batter in by spoonfuls. Fry until golden brown; remove with slotted spoon. Drain on paper towels. Serve hot. Makes 36 to 48 balls.

southern-fried vegetables

These are delicious finger foods.

Cauliflower, cut into florets
Squash, sliced thin
Eggplant, sliced thin
Okra, with stems removed

Salt and pepper to taste
Flour or cornmeal
Deep fat for frying

Shake prepared vegetables in seasoned flour or cornmeal until well-coated.
Heat fat in skillet; fry vegetables until all are golden brown. Drain on paper towels and serve at once. Makes a lot.

pickled okra

Make these in quantity, because you'll want to serve them often—and they're easy to put together.

8 cups vinegar
8 cups water
1 cup salt
Several pounds fresh okra,
   washed, stems cut off

1 teaspoon dillseed
2 cloves garlic, chopped
2 small hot peppers, chopped

Boil vinegar, water, and salt together about 10 minutes. While this is boiling, place prepared okra in pint jars. Divide dill, garlic, and peppers so that some of each are on top of each jar of okra. Pour hot liquid into jars. Allow to cool; seal. Put jars aside at least 3 weeks for pickling process to take place.
Chill pickled okra before serving. Makes about 10 pints.

toasted pecans

A Southerner puts the accent on the first syllable of the word pecan, but, however you say it, those nuts are great! Toast the full quantity given below—you won't be sorry. They go fast.

12 cups pecans
¼ pound butter

Salt

Place pecans in rectangular oven dish. Toast in 250°F oven 30 minutes. Add butter over all by slicing or dotting it over nuts. Stir once or twice, until pecans and butter have mixed well. Nuts will be greasy at this point. Sprinkle generously with salt. Toast pecans 1 hour more, salting again several times; stir as you go. When done, butter will be completely absorbed and nuts crisp. Makes lots.

soups

one-hour black-eyed pea soup

1 10-ounce package frozen
   black-eyed peas
1 cup diced ham
1 large onion, diced

Dash of hot red pepper
½ teaspoon salt
4 cups water
¼ cup dry wine (optional)

Combine all ingredients in large saucepan in order given. Bring to boil, then reduce to simmer. Cook about 1 hour or until peas are tender. Add water if necessary.

If you like the wine addition, add another ¼ cup 5 minutes before serving. Makes 4 to 6 servings.

virginia clam chowder

12 large clams, boiled,
   removed from shells
¼ pound fat bacon
2 medium onions, sliced fine

3 medium potatoes, diced
Salt and pepper to taste
2 tablespoons cornmeal
1 cup light cream

Chop clams fine; set aside. Reserve liquid, adding enough water to make 6 cups.

Cut bacon into small pieces; fry crisp and brown; use large, heavy saucepan. Add onions, potatoes, clams, and liquid; simmer until potatoes are fork-tender. Season with salt and pepper to taste. Remove ¼ cup broth from saucepan; mix with cornmeal. Stir back into chowder. Add cream; heat all until tongue-hot but not boiling. Serve at once. Makes 4 to 6 servings.

corn chowder

3 slices bacon, chopped
3 tablespoons chopped onion
1¼ cups peeled and diced potatoes
1 cup water
2 cups (16-ounce can) cream-style corn
3 cups milk
½ teaspoon salt

Cook bacon in heavy pot until crisp. Remove from pan; save for later use.

Lightly brown onion in bacon fat. Add potatoes and water; boil gently 10 minutes. Add corn; cook 10 minutes longer. Stir in milk, salt, and bacon. Heat until just hot. Serve at once. Makes 4 to 6 servings.

okra soup

1 large soup bone, with meat on it
3 quarts water
2 medium onions, chopped
2 pounds fresh okra, sliced ¼ inch thick
Salt, pepper, and bay leaf
3 or 4 slices bacon
8 large fresh tomatoes or 2 No. 2½ cans tomatoes

Cook meat in water 2 hours. Add remaining ingredients in order given. Cook on low flame another 2 hours. Add water by the cupful, if needed.

Fifteen minutes before serving, remove bone and bay leaf. Cut any large pieces of meat to bite-size. Return meat to soup; simmer until ready to dish up. Makes 10 to 12 servings.

cream of pumpkin soup

Many Southerners consider this only as a cold soup. If this is your preference, chill soup, then garnish when ready to serve. It is tasty either way.

½ cup diced onion
2 tablespoons butter
2 cups chicken stock
2 cups canned pumpkin (1 16-ounce can)
1 teaspoon cinnamon (be generous)
1 tablespoon sugar
½ cup cream for soup or sour cream for garnish

Sauté onion and butter in medium-size heavy saucepan until onion is transparent. Add 1 cup soup stock; simmer until onion is tender. Stir in canned pumpkin, blending until smooth. Add remaining stock, cinnamon, and sugar; stir until all flavors blend. Last, add cream; serve when hot.

If you prefer sour-cream garnish, eliminate the cream and top each soup bowl with a generous spoonful of sour cream. Makes 3 to 4 servings.

new orleans onion soup

2 cups onions, sliced into rings
3 tablespoons butter
1 quart chicken stock (beef may be used)
½ cup dry sherry (optional)
6 slices toast
Grated Parmesan cheese

new orleans onion soup

Sauté onions in butter until quite soft and even a little brown around edges. Add soup stock; simmer, uncovered, 30 minutes. Add dry sherry; stir well.

Ladle soup into soup bowls. Top each with slice of toast; cover with Parmesan cheese. If you have used flameproof soup dishes, put under broiler until cheese melts. Serve at once. Makes 4 to 6 servings.

shrimp soup

1 pound raw shrimp,
   shelled, deveined
Cayenne pepper to taste
Salt to taste
2 tablespoons flour
2 tablespoons oil

1 large onion, chopped fine
1 clove garlic, chopped fine
2 cups water
1 cup cooked rice
1 tablespoon chopped fresh parsley

Sprinkle raw shrimp generously with cayenne and salt; set aside.

Make dark-brown roux with flour and oil. (Stir together over medium flame until dark. Roux is typically Louisiana south.) Brown onion and garlic in roux. Add shrimp. When shrimp are pink, add water. Cover; simmer about 45 minutes.

Five minutes before serving, add rice and parsley. Add additional seasonings if needed. Spoon into soup dishes. Makes 4 servings.

oyster stew

1 pint oysters
4 tablespoons butter
½ teaspoon salt
Pepper to taste
Dash of Tabasco sauce

1 pint milk
1 pint light cream
2 teaspoons butter
Paprika

Drain oysters; reserve liquor. Melt 4 tablespoons butter in heavy saucepan, adding salt, pepper, and Tabasco. Add reserved liquor to pot; stir to blend well. Add oysters; cook only until edges begin to curl, about 3 to 5 minutes. Stir in milk and cream; bring to boil, but do not boil.

Spoon soup into hot bowls. Dot each bowl with butter and a healthy dash of paprika. Makes 4 servings.

11

fresh tomato soup

fresh tomato soup

Since Southern gardens are full of fresh vegetables, this soup is best with freshly picked produce.

6 medium-size tomatoes
1 onion, chopped
1 stalk celery, chopped
2 cups chicken broth
1 tablespoon tomato paste

½ teaspoon dried basil
¼ teaspoon freshly ground pepper
½ teaspoon salt
½ cup sour cream

Cut tomatoes into wedges; place in 1½-quart saucepan with all ingredients except sour cream. Simmer, uncovered, 30 minutes. Strain to remove tomato skins and seeds. Adjust seasonings. Garnish with spoonfuls of sour cream. Makes 6 servings.

catfish gumbo

1 pound skinned catfish fillets or
   fish fillets of your choice,
   fresh or frozen
½ cup chopped celery
½ cup chopped green pepper
½ cup chopped onion
1 clove garlic, finely chopped
¼ cup melted fat or oil
2 cups beef stock

1 1-pound can tomatoes
1 10-ounce package frozen
   okra, sliced
2 teaspoons salt
¼ teaspoon pepper
¼ teaspoon thyme
1 whole bay leaf
Dash liquid hot-pepper sauce
1½ cups hot cooked rice

Cut fillets into 1-inch pieces.

Cook celery, green pepper, onion, and garlic in fat until tender.
Add beef stock, tomatoes, okra, and seasonings. Cover; simmer 30
minutes. Add fish. Cover; simmer 15 minutes longer or until fish
flakes easily when tested with fork. Remove bay leaf.

Place ¼ cup rice in each soup bowl. Fill with gumbo; serve at
once. Makes 6 servings.

lazy-man's corn gumbo

A lazy man or woman uses all the modern conveniences, and that's
what this recipe does. Quick and easy, but good, too.

1 tablespoon butter
1 small onion, diced
2 10-ounce cans chicken gumbo soup
1 16-ounce can creamed corn with liquid
2 cups milk

Melt butter in soup pot; brown onion around edges. Add remaining
ingredients, stirring to blend flavors. Simmer about 10 minutes or
until liquid is hot but not boiling. Serve at once. Makes 6 to 8
servings.

cream of peanut soup

1 medium onion, chopped
2 celery ribs, chopped
4 tablespoons butter
3 tablespoons flour
2 quarts chicken stock (canned will do)
2 cups peanut butter
1¾ cups light cream
Chopped peanuts for garnish

Stir onion and celery in large pot with butter until vegetables are
soft but not brown. Blend in flour; stir until smooth. Add chicken
stock, still stirring; bring to boil. (The onion and celery may be
strained out at this point if you prefer. Not necessary, however.)
Remove from heat. Add peanut butter and cream; blend together
until smooth. Return to low heat (do not boil) 5 minutes.

Serve soup topped with chopped peanuts. Makes 10 to 12 servings.

egg delights

baked eggs and artichokes

Prepare this well ahead of the day you want it and freeze it. Before the company comes, thaw it, then rewarm it for 20 minutes in a 350°F oven. You'll love it.

3 or 4 green onions
2 6½-ounce jars artichoke hearts
2 tablespoons oil
1 clove garlic, halved
4 eggs, beaten
8 ounces cheddar cheese, grated
6 saltine crackers, crushed

Mince onions fine, using some green tops. Cut artichokes in thirds. If marinated in oil, reserve 2 tablespoons oil.

Sauté onions and garlic in oil. Remove garlic. Combine all ingredients together in bowl. Place in greased 8-inch Pyrex dish. Bake at 350°F 40 minutes.

Cut into squares; serve at once. Makes 4 to 6 servings.

bacon and egg cake

½ pound bacon
6 eggs
1 tablespoon flour
½ teaspoon salt
½ cup milk or cream
3 tablespoons finely cut chives

Cut each bacon slice in half. Fry lightly, not too crisp. Drain; set aside. Remove all but about 1 tablespoon fat from skillet.

Combine eggs, flour, and salt in bowl. Gradually add milk.

Warm fat in skillet over moderate heat. Pour in egg mixture; turn heat to low. Do not stir. Let eggs set firm. This takes about 20 minutes. When mixture is firm, remove from heat.

Arrange bacon slices and chives on top. Serve directly from the pan. Makes 4 servings.

rice cakes creole

Leftover ham and rice become a gourmet pleasure when tossed together like this.

2 cups cooked rice
1 cup fairly finely diced cooked ham
1 tablespoon green pepper
2 eggs, beaten slightly
¼ teaspoon instant minced onion
¼ teaspoon dry mustard
Fat for frying

Mix ingredients together. Drop by tablespoons into greased skillet to make 2-inch cakes. When browned on one side, turn; brown other side.

Once fried, these rice cakes may be frozen and reheated later. Makes 4 to 6 servings.

scrambled country corn

6 slices lean bacon, diced
1 medium onion, chopped
1 green pepper, chopped
2 cups corn kernels, fresh preferred, but canned may be used
1 large tomato, chopped
6 eggs
1 teaspoon Worcestershire sauce
1 teaspoon salt
Dash of freshly ground pepper

Cook bacon in deep skillet until almost crisp. Pour off excess fat. Add onion, green pepper, corn, and tomato. Sauté until onion is transparent.

Beat eggs and seasonings in bowl until light and frothy. Stir into skillet vegetables; stir until eggs are set.

Serve this with your favorite sweet rolls. Makes 4 to 6 servings.

eggs in a nest

2 cups cold mashed potatoes
5 tablespoons hot milk
½ cup chopped ham or
    fried bacon bits
3 tablespoons chopped parsley
4 eggs
Salt and pepper to taste
1 tablespoon butter

Soften mashed potatoes with hot milk. Add ham and parsley; mix well. Place in greased baking dish. With back of tablespoon, form 4 large hollows on top for eggs. Break 1 egg into each hollow. Sprinkle with salt and pepper; dot with butter. Bake at 325°F about 12 minutes or until egg whites are firm. Serve at once. Makes 4 servings.

rice pancakes

4 tablespoons butter, melted
3 whole eggs, beaten
2 cups cooked rice
2 teaspoons baking powder
1 teaspoon salt
1 cup flour
¼ cup milk or cream
Shortening for frying

Mix ingredients in order given, adding milk to batter last.

Heat shortening in skillet. Drop batter by tablespoons into hot fat. When golden brown on one side, turn pancake. Add extra shortening if needed.

Serve rice pancakes with apricot preserves. Makes about 6 servings.

green eggs

The name may remind you of Dr. Seuss—*Green Eggs and Ham*—but there is no ham, and the taste is delicious.

3 cups cooked or canned greens
Salt and pepper to taste
3 tablespoons butter
6 eggs
½ cup shredded cheese

Drain liquid from greens into pan. Cook liquid until only a little is left. Add greens, salt, pepper, and butter; bring to boil. Break eggs on top of greens; sprinkle with cheese. Cover; cook very slowly until eggs are firm and cheese is melted. Makes 6 servings.

eggs supreme

1 cup grated American cheese
2 tablespoons butter
1 cup light cream
½ teaspoon salt
Dash of freshly ground pepper
1 teaspoon prepared mustard
6 eggs, slightly beaten

Spread cheese in greased 8-inch-square baking dish. Dot with butter.

Combine cream, salt, pepper, and mustard. Pour half over cheese, followed by beaten eggs. Add rest of cream mixture. Bake at 325°F about 40 minutes or until set and firm. Makes 4 to 6 servings.

spinach and egg bake

4 tablespoons flour
Dash of cayenne pepper
1 teaspoon salt
4 tablespoons butter, melted
1½ cups milk
1 cup bread crumbs or cracker meal
2 10-ounce packages frozen chopped spinach, cooked, drained
2 hard-cooked eggs, peeled, sliced thin
1 cup grated cheddar cheese
1 strip bacon, cut into 1-inch lengths

Add flour, cayenne and salt to melted butter. Gradually stir in milk over low heat until mixture is slightly thickened and smooth.

In 1½-quart greased baking dish, layer half of bread crumbs, half of spinach, slices of 1 egg, ⅓ of sauce, and half of cheese. Repeat layering with spinach, egg, ⅓ sauce, and remaining cheese. Pour on rest of sauce; top with rest of bread crumbs, then bacon bits. Bake at 350°F 40 to 45 minutes. Makes 4 to 6 servings.

strawberry omelet

This makes any brunch a delicious party—and, since you use frozen fruit, it is available all year round.

2 cups frozen whole strawberries
1 tablespoon sugar
4 eggs, separated
½ teaspoon salt
1 tablespoon lemon juice
1 tablespoon butter

Sprinkle strawberries with sugar; let stand 2 hours to thaw.

Beat egg whites until you can turn bowl upside down and they don't fall out. That's Grandmother's way of saying beat egg whites stiff.

Beat egg yolks with salt and lemon juice. Fold into stiffly beaten egg whites until no yellow streaks remain.

Melt butter in medium skillet that can go into oven. Pour in egg mixture; tilt pan to coat sides. Cook over low heat just 5 minutes. When mixture is set on bottom, bake at 350°F 5 minutes more.

Lift omelet onto heated plate; spoon strawberry mixture over it. Cut in pie wedges to serve. Makes 4 to 6 servings.

sour-cream and ham pie

5 eggs, separated, whites beaten stiff
1 cup sour cream
¼ teaspoon salt
1 cup finely chopped cooked ham
2 tablespoons butter

Beat egg yolks until well-mixed. Add half the sour cream and salt. Fold in stiffly beaten egg whites and ham.

Heat butter in medium-size skillet. Gently pour in omelet mixture. Cook over low heat about 5 minutes. Place skillet in 325°F oven; cook about 12 minutes more. Top should be golden brown and firm.

Slice pie into wedges; garnish each slice with sour cream. Makes 4 to 6 servings.

meat

barbecued brisket

This could be called plain stew or ragout, but the flavor makes it special.

1 onion, diced
1 clove garlic, diced
2 pounds brisket, cut into 1-inch pieces
½ pound mushrooms, sliced
½ cup beef stock
½ cup barbecue sauce
1 tablespoon cornstarch (optional)

Place onion, garlic, and mushrooms in heavy baking dish. Top with meat; add stock and barbecue sauce. Bake at 300°F about 3 hours, until meat is fork-tender. Remove fat from gravy.

If you prefer slightly thickened gravy, remove 1 cup gravy from pot; mix with 1 tablespoon cornstarch. Return to pot; stir until slightly thickened.

Serve brisket with hot buttered noodles or over rice. Makes 4 to 6 servings.

seven-layer casserole

This is a meal in itself and is so good!

1 cup uncooked rice
1 cup cooked, whole-kernel corn
Salt and pepper to taste
2 cups (15-ounce can) tomato sauce
¾ cup water
½ cup finely chopped onion
½ cup finely chopped green pepper
1 cup cooked or canned green beans
¾ pound ground beef
4 slices bacon, cut up

Put rice and corn in baking dish. Sprinkle with salt and pepper.
Mix tomato sauce and water. Pour half of mixture over corn and rice. Add layers of onion, green pepper, green beans, and beef. Sprinkle with salt and pepper. Add rest of tomato-sauce mixture. Top with bacon. Cover tightly. Bake at 350°F 1 hour. Uncover; cook 30 minutes longer. Makes 4 to 6 servings.

grits croquettes

2 cups cooked grits
2 cups finely chopped meat, chicken, or fish
2 tablespoons chopped onion
1 teaspoon salt
Pepper to taste
1 teaspoon Worcestershire sauce
1 cup dry bread crumbs
1 egg, beaten
Oil for deep frying

Combine grits, meat, onion, salt, pepper, and Worcestershire sauce in bowl. Chill thoroughly. Shape mixture into balls or other shape, making 12 croquettes. Roll balls in bread crumbs; dip in egg; roll again in bread crumbs. Cook croquettes in heated oil, turning once to brown each side. Drain and serve. Makes 6 servings.

quick ground-beef gumbo

1 large onion, sliced
1 tablespoon shortening
1½ pounds ground beef
1 can chicken-gumbo soup (condensed)
1 teaspoon salt
¼ teaspoon freshly ground black pepper

Tan onion in hot shortening. Add ground beef, stirring until all is browned. Add can of soup (as is, without extra water), salt, and pepper. Simmer about 5 minutes or until all flavors blend.
Serve gumbo on toasted hamburger rolls. Makes 4 to 6 servings.

beef round over noodles

beef round over noodles

2 tablespoons shortening
1 teaspoon soy sauce
½ teaspoon sugar
2 teaspoons sherry
3 cups thinly sliced onions
2 teaspoons cornstarch
1 tablespoon soy sauce
1½ pounds beef round, cut into 1-inch pieces
1 tablespoon Worcestershire sauce
1 teaspoon garlic salt

Heat shortening in large skillet with 1 teaspoon soy sauce, sugar, and 1 teaspoon sherry. Sauté onions in this.

Mix cornstarch, 1 tablespoon soy sauce, and 1 teaspoon sherry in bowl. Dredge meat in mixture, coating every piece. Put dredged meat in onions; brown. Stir in Worcestershire sauce and garlic salt. Cover; let simmer 1 hour. This meat draws its own gravy, but you may want to stir occasionally while it cooks.

Serve on a bed of noodles and enjoy. Makes 4 to 6 servings.

ham potato cakes

These are sure to go fast because they are so good. A good way to use up leftover ham, too.

1 cup mashed potatoes
1 cup finely ground cooked ham
1 egg, slightly beaten
¼ cup minced or grated onion
¼ teaspoon dry mustard
¼ teaspoon lemon pepper
Flour for batter
Fat for frying

Mix together potatoes, ham, egg, onion, and seasonings. Form into flat cakes about 3 inches in diameter. Dip each cake lightly in flour, coating both sides. Set aside.

Melt fat in medium-size skillet. Lightly brown each cake on both sides. Drain on paper towels; put on warming plate in oven until all are cooked and ready to serve. Makes 4 to 6 servings.

pork chops and sweet potatoes

4 center-cut pork chops
Salt and pepper to taste
¼ cup flour
2 tablespoons butter
½ cup currant jelly
½ cup orange juice
1 tablespoon lemon juice
1 teaspoon dry mustard
1 teaspoon paprika
½ teaspoon ground ginger
3 to 4 medium sweet potatoes, boiled, sliced

Season chops with salt and pepper; coat with flour. Brown on both sides.

Melt butter in small saucepan. Add remaining ingredients, except sweet potatoes, stirring constantly, to make sauce.

Arrange sweet potatoes and pork chops in oven-to-table dish. Pour over ¾ of sauce; keep remainder for basting while baking. Bake, uncovered, at 350°F 45 minutes. Makes 4 servings.

20

glazed ham and rice loaf

This could be used for a company dinner despite the fact that it's actually just another way to use leftover ham. When it's all done, the cook won't be worn out with fussing, either.

1½ pounds cooked ham, ground
1½ cups cooked white rice
1½ cups soft bread crumbs
1½ teaspoons dry mustard
1½ cups milk
4 eggs, beaten light and frothy

glaze
½ cup currant jelly
⅓ cup prepared mustard

In large bowl mix all ingredients except glaze; make a high rounded loaf. Place in 13 × 9 × 2-inch baking dish. Bake, uncovered, at 350°F 50 minutes.

Prepare glaze by thoroughly mixing jelly and mustard together until pasty and smooth.

After ham loaf has baked 50 minutes, brush it liberally all over with glaze. Bake, uncovered, 20 minutes more or until glaze is "glistening brown." Let cool 20 minutes before slicing. Makes 6 to 8 servings.

ham shortcake

1 cup diced leftover ham
3 tablespoons bacon drippings
¼ cup flour
2½ cups milk
¼ teaspoon mustard
½ teaspoon salt
Dash of celery salt (optional)
4 hard-boiled eggs, cut into fourths
Hot biscuits

Brown ham slightly in drippings. Stir in flour. Add milk gradually; cook and stir until slightly thickened. Stir in mustard, salt, and celery salt. Add eggs; heat just until hot, stirring only to keep from sticking. Spoon over hot split biscuits. Makes 6 to 8 servings.

country ham with redeye gravy

Be sure to include hot grits or hot biscuits in your dinner menu to absorb this gravy.

6 ham slices about ½ inch thick
¾ cup strong black coffee

Fry ham slices, 1 or 2 at a time, depending on skillet size, over medium-high heat. Fry 5 to 6 minutes per side. When done, remove ham to heated platter.

Pour off all but about 3 tablespoons fat in skillet. Brown remaining drippings. Add coffee, being sure to scrape up pan scrapings (these are the redeyes); bring to boil. Gravy may be spooned over ham or served separately in gravy boat. Makes 6 servings.

hoppin' john

Some people hop around the table on one foot before they sit down to eat this. Others consider Hoppin' John good-luck fare for New Year's Day. Whichever, this casserole only improves with reheating.

2 cups dried black-eyed peas
1 large onion, diced
¼ teaspoon hot red pepper
5 cups water
¼ cup dry wine (optional)
1½ pounds smoked boneless pork shoulder butt
4 medium potatoes, peeled, quartered

Place peas, onion, hot red pepper, water, and wine in large pot. Bring to rolling boil. Add pork. Cover; bring to boil again. Simmer about 2 hours, until meat and peas are tender. Add more water as needed. Add potatoes during last half hour of cooking. Check water; add more if needed. Allow to cool; refrigerate overnight. Remove fat from top.

Fill casserole with peas and potatoes. Layer sliced meat on top; heat in 400°F oven 30 minutes or so, until hot through. Makes 6 servings.

hoppin' john

pan-fried lamb slices

1 leg of lamb
2 or 3 medium onions, peeled, sliced into rings
4 or more tablespoons oil for frying
Salt and pepper to taste

With sharp knife cut lamb into ½-inch slices.

Brown onion rings in oil in large skillet. Drain; set aside to keep warm.

Fry meat slices in same oil; season with salt and pepper.

To serve, arrange meat on platter. Cover slices with drained onions. Add mashed potatoes and a salad and dinner is ready. Makes 8 to 10 servings.

veal delight

4 veal chops
Salt and pepper to taste
4 tablespoons butter
½ pound mushrooms, sliced
4 tablespoons minced onion
2 cups catsup
4 teaspoons currant jelly
4 tablespoons dry sherry

Trim chops; season liberally with salt and pepper.

Melt 2 tablespoons butter in heavy skillet, sauté mushrooms, stirring constantly, 3 minutes. Remove; set aside.

Brown chops on both sides; set aside.

Melt remaining butter in skillet; lightly tan onion. Add catsup, currant jelly, and sherry. Bring to boil; simmer 30 minutes. Add chops; simmer 1 hour, basting occasionally. Add mushrooms 10 minutes before serving. Makes 4 servings.

baked pork tenderloin

Butterfly pork chops can be substituted if you can't get tenderloins.

½ cup flour
6 to 8 pork tenderloins
1 cup chopped onion
1 clove garlic, minced
1 teaspoon ground ginger
1 1-pound can applesauce
½ cup sauterne wine
½ cup soy sauce

Flour pork on both sides. Brown pork, onion, garlic, and ginger in skillet.

Mix together applesauce, wine, and soy sauce; pour over pork. Stir together to blend flavors. Remove from skillet; place in oven dish. Cook at least 1 hour at 350°F.

Serve pork with mashed potatoes and a salad for a dinner delight. Makes 6 servings.

batter-dipped hot dogs

Serve this with your favorite salad for a quick-and-easy supper.

½ cup cornmeal
½ cup flour
1 teaspoon salt
½ teaspoon pepper
½ cup milk
1 egg, beaten
2 tablespoons oil
12 hot dogs
Fat or oil for deep frying

Mix cornmeal, flour, salt, and pepper in bowl. Add milk, egg, and oil. Stir until smooth. Dip hot dogs into batter; drain over bowl. Fry in deep fat 2 to 3 minutes, until golden brown, turning once. Remove from fat; drain. Makes 6 servings.

poultry

barbecued chicken

This barbecue is for when you can't use the outdoor grill.

1 2½- to 3-pound frying chicken, cut into serving pieces

Disjoint chicken; place in casserole dish with cover.

sauce
2 tablespoons butter
1 cup catsup
½ cup chili sauce
1 teaspoon dry mustard
Dash of Tabasco sauce
⅓ cup vinegar
2 teaspoons Worcestershire sauce
3 tablespoons brown sugar
1 medium onion, grated

Place ingredients in saucepan in order given; bring to boil. Simmer 5 minutes, until all flavors blend.

Pour sauce over chicken. If possible, marinate several hours.

Cover casserole; bake at 350°F 1½ hours. Uncover for last 15 minutes of baking. Makes 4 to 6 servings.

fried chicken with cream gravy

No Southern cookbook is complete without fried chicken, and there are as many recipes as there are cooks. This is only one of them, albeit a very tasty dish.

Salt, pepper, and garlic salt
1 cup flour
2½- to 3-pound frying chicken, cut into serving pieces
Fat for deep frying

Mix seasonings with flour; coat each chicken piece with this.
Heat fat in skillet; fry chicken a few pieces at a time. Cook about 25 minutes per batch of chicken, so that pieces are crisp and crusty. Drain on paper towels; set on warmed platter.

cream gravy
2 tablespoons cornstarch
¾ cup hot chicken broth
½ cup milk at room temperature
1 teaspoon salt
¼ teaspoon pepper

Pour off most of fat in skillet, leaving about 2 tablespoons. Mix cornstarch with chicken broth. Add to hot fat, stirring constantly. Gradually add milk, salt, and pepper. When slightly thickened, gravy is ready.
Put gravy in gravy boat; serve with chicken. Makes 4 to 6 servings.

chicken and biscuits

If you're a biscuit-maker, make your own. If you need a shortcut, use the kind that come in ready-made packages.

1 stewing chicken, cut up
½ cup coarsely chopped celery
1 small onion, quartered
1 teaspoon salt
½ teaspoon pepper
4 cups water
4 tablespoons flour mixed with 6 tablespoons water to form a paste
2 packages prepared biscuits

Simmer chicken, celery, onion, and seasonings in water about 1 hour. When chicken is tender, remove bones and skin; cut into medium-size pieces.
Thicken 2½ cups stock with flour paste; add salt and pepper as needed.
Arrange chicken in 13 × 9 × 2-inch baking dish. Cover with gravy; allow to cool to room temperature. Place biscuits on top of chicken and gravy. Bake at 350°F 30 minutes or until biscuits are browned on top. Makes 6 to 8 servings.

mustard-fried chicken

This recipe gives a delicious different taste to fried chicken.

2 or more tablespoons dry mustard
¼ cup water
2½- to 3-pound frying chicken, cut into serving pieces
Flour seasoned with salt and pepper
Fat for frying
1 can condensed cream of celery soup
1 cup plus 2 tablespoons milk
1 can condensed tomato soup

Mix dry mustard with water to form thick paste. Spread paste liberally over chicken pieces. Dredge chicken with flour.

Heat fat in large skillet; cook chicken on all sides until golden brown. Remove from skillet.

Reduce fat in skillet to about 3 tablespoons. Add celery soup, milk, and tomato soup; mix well. Replace chicken in gravy; cover skillet. Simmer 30 minutes, until chicken is tender. Makes 4 to 6 servings.

chicken gumbo

⅓ cup flour
⅓ cup melted fat
1 onion, finely chopped
1 large chicken, cut into serving pieces
6 cups hot water
Salt and pepper to taste

Mix flour with hot fat in large pan. Cook and stir over low heat until flour is browned. (This is a "roux.") Add onion; cook until tender, about 5 minutes. Add chicken; stir until chicken is lightly browned. Add water, salt, and pepper; mix well with roux. Cover pan; heat quickly to boiling. Lower heat; cook until chicken is tender, about 45 minutes.

Serve chicken over hot cooked rice. Makes 6 servings.

brunswick stew

This is one of those recipes made all over the South, with as many variations as there are cooks. Add your own touches to this basic stew—anything goes.

1 medium onion, chopped
1 tablespoon oil
2 cups cooked tomatoes
2 cups cooked lima beans
2 cups cooked corn
1 cup cooked okra
2 cups diced chicken or turkey
Salt and pepper to taste

Brown onion in large pan with oil.

Drain vegetables (canned may be substituted for fresh); reserve liquid. Add water to liquid to make 2 cups. Add liquid to onions, followed by rest of ingredients. Heat just to boiling; simmer 5 minutes. Serve at once. Makes 4 to 6 servings.

chicken breasts in sour cream

chicken breasts in sour cream

1 package dried chipped beef
6 chicken breasts, boned, skinned, split
6 slices bacon, cut in half
2 cans condensed mushroom soup
1 pint sour cream

Chop beef finely; place in bottom of casserole dish.

Wrap each chicken piece with half-slice of bacon. Place each piece on its own bed of chipped beef.

Mix together undiluted soup and sour cream; pour over chicken. Bake at 275°F 2½ to 3 hours.

Serve chicken on bed of hot rice or mashed potatoes covered with the good gravy. Makes 6 servings.

baked chicken livers

Save all your chicken livers for this one. Once you make it, you'll want to make it again and again.

3 or 4 medium-size onions, sliced ¼ inch thick
10 or 12 chicken livers
3 strips bacon
Salt and pepper to taste
½ cup sherry

Arrange onion slices in flat oblong baking dish. Put 1 chicken liver on top of each onion; salt lightly.

Cut each bacon strip into quarters, and place one quarter on each chicken liver. Sprinkle with salt and pepper. Pour sherry over all. Bake at 350°F about 45 minutes or until bacon is crisp. Baste occasionally during baking time. Serve 2 or 3 livers per portion. Makes 4 servings.

creamed chicken and ham

Serve this proudly over cornbread squares or hot waffles. It's a winner and easy, too.

1½ tablespoons flour or cornstarch
1½ tablespoons butter
¾ cup chicken stock
¼ cup cream
½ cup diced cooked chicken
½ cup diced cooked ham
¼ cup chopped celery
1 tablespoon parsley
1 egg, beaten
1 or 2 tablespoons sherry (optional)

Add flour to melted butter; stir until blended. Slowly stir in soup stock, then cream. When sauce is smooth and to boiling point, add chicken, ham, celery, and parsley.

Remove 2 tablespoons sauce; mix with beaten egg. Reduce heat to low; return egg mixture to heat. Stir constantly until all thickens slightly.

If you like, add 1 or 2 tablespoons sherry just before serving. Makes 4 servings.

chicken croquettes

4 cups cooked chicken, put through meat grinder
1 cup chopped celery
1 tablespoon grated onion
4 tablespoons butter
4 tablespoons flour
1 cup milk
1 teaspoon salt
Generous dash of freshly ground pepper
1 egg, beaten with 1 tablespoon milk
1 cup cracker meal
Oil for deep frying
2 cans cream of mushroom soup for quick sauce

Mix chicken and celery in large bowl; set aside.

In small saucepan sauté onion in butter until onion is transparent. Blend in flour. Add milk; heat, stirring constantly. When slightly thickened, add salt and pepper; simmer just 3 minutes. Add sauce to chicken and celery, and chill several hours.

Shape chicken into rolls about 3 inches long. Dip into beaten egg; roll in cracker meal. Place croquettes on waxed-paper-lined baking sheet; chill in refrigerator at least 3 hours more.

Fry croquettes in deep fat, a few at a time, until brown on all sides. Drain on paper towels. These may be kept warm in very low (250°F) oven until ready to serve.

For a quick sauce with the croquettes, heat cream of mushroom soup over low heat, stirring until piping hot. If you prefer a thinner sauce, add milk by ¼ cups and stir until desired consistency is reached. Makes 4 to 6 servings.

chicken in lemon–dill butter

chicken in lemon–dill butter

This is rich, but so good.

¼ pound butter
2 tablespoons lemon juice
1 teaspoon salt
1 clove garlic, minced
½ teaspoon paprika
1 can sliced mushrooms, drained
1 tablespoon dillweed
2½- to 3-pound frying chicken, cut into serving pieces

Melt butter in large skillet. Add all ingredients, except chicken, in order given; bring to boil. Add chicken; again bring to boil, but do not actually boil. Cover skillet. Lower heat; simmer 30 minutes or until chicken is tender.

Remove chicken to platter; serve with noodles or rice, over which you pour the remaining liquid. Makes 4 to 6 servings.

batter-fried chicken breasts

6 to 8 whole chicken breasts, boned
2 teaspoons salt
Dash of pepper

batter
1 egg, lightly beaten
½ cup milk
2 tablespoons flour

1½ cups flour for dredging chicken
Oil for deep-fat frying

Divide each chicken breast in half to make 12 to 16 pieces. Sprinkle each piece with salt and pepper.

Mix egg and milk in shallow bowl or pie dish. Add flour; mix until very smooth.

Dip each piece of chicken in batter, then dredge generously in flour.

Put 4 or 5 chicken pieces into preheated oil; deep fry 12 to 15 minutes or until chicken is golden brown on all sides. Drain on paper towels; keep warm in very low oven until all chicken is fried. Makes 4 to 6 servings.

pecan chicken salad

4 cups chicken, cooked, diced
1 cup finely chopped celery
1 tablespoon finely chopped sweet pickle
1 cup chopped pecans
1½ teaspoons salt
Dash (be generous) of freshly ground pepper
¾ cup mayonnaise
¼ cup stock from cooked chicken

Mix chicken, celery, pickle, and pecans in large bowl. Season with salt and pepper to taste.

Dilute mayonnaise with stock; stir until well-blended. Add mayonnaise to chicken; stir all together. Cover. Refrigerate salad—it's well to put it together in the morning for lunch. When ready to serve, stir once again to be sure the dressing has covered all. Makes 4 to 6 servings.

turkey surprise

This is a particularly pleasant way to finish off a holiday turkey.

2 tablespoons butter
2 cups cooked rice (Wild rice is always good!)
1 pound pork sausage
3 cups diced leftover turkey
2 cans cream of mushroom soup, undiluted
1 can button mushrooms

Add butter to rice; set aside.

Sauté sausage in medium skillet, draining off excess fat.

Place layer each of sausage, turkey, rice, soup, and mushrooms in 2-quart casserole. Bake at 400°F 20 minutes or until lightly brown on top. Makes 6 servings.

seafood

lemon flounder

2 large flounder
½ lemon, sliced thin
¾ tablespoon poultry seasoning
Salt and pepper
2 tablespoons lemon juice
1 tablespoon chopped parsley
3 spring onions, diced, including greens
¼ pound melted butter

Score flounder with sharp knife. Lay lemon slices in slits.

Add remaining ingredients to melted butter; simmer 3 minutes.

Place flounder in ungreased oven dish. Pour sauce over fish. Broil flounder about 20 minutes or until fish is flaky to a fork. Baste several times with sauce while fish is cooking. Makes 4 to 6 servings.

dixieland catfish

6 skinned, pan-dressed catfish or other fish, fresh or frozen
½ cup French dressing
12 thin lemon slices
Paprika

Clean, wash, and dry fish, or thaw frozen fish. Brush inside and out with French dressing.

Cut 6 lemon slices in half. Place 2 halves in each body cavity. Place fish in well-greased baking dish, 13 × 9 × 2 inches. Place lemon slice on each fish. Brush top of fish with remaining French dressing. Sprinkle with paprika. Bake at 350°F 30 to 35 minutes, until fish is fork-tender. Serve at once. Makes 6 servings.

new orleans fish steaks

2 pounds fish steaks, fresh or frozen
½ teaspoon salt
Dash of freshly ground pepper
2 cups cooked rice
2 tablespoons grated onion
½ teaspoon curry powder
6 thin lemon slices
4 tablespoons butter
Chopped parsley

Cut steaks into serving-size portions; place in well-greased baking dish, 13 × 9 × 2 inches. Sprinkle with salt and pepper.

Combine rice, onion, and curry powder. Spread over fish. Top with lemon slices; dot with butter. Cover. Bake in moderate (350°F) oven 25 to 35 minutes or until fish flakes easily when tested with fork. Remove cover last few minutes of cooking to allow slight browning. Sprinkle with parsley. Makes 6 servings.

fast bouillabaisse

2 cups canned tomatoes, drained (1-pound can)
2 tablespoons butter
1½ cups diced celery
2 medium onions, sliced
1 pound frozen fish fillets, cut into bite-size pieces
1 teaspoon salt
¼ teaspoon black pepper
2 cups canned potatoes, drained, quartered
2 cups chicken stock
Parsley for garnish

Put tomatoes and butter in medium saucepan; bring to boil. Add celery and onions; simmer until onions are soft, 3 to 5 minutes. Add fish, salt, pepper, and potatoes, stirring once. Last, put in soup stock. Bring to boil; reduce heat to simmer. Simmer 10 minutes.

Garnish bouillabaisse with parsley; serve. Makes 4 to 6 servings.

fish fillets in sour cream

1 pound fish fillets
Salt and pepper to taste
Dash of Tabasco sauce
1 cup sour cream
2 tablespoons finely chopped dill pickle
2 tablespoons minced onion
2 tablespoons chopped green pepper
1 tablespoon chopped parsley
1 tablespoon lemon juice
¼ teaspoon dry mustard
¼ teaspoon sweet basil
Paprika

Place fish in greased baking dish. Sprinkle generously with salt and pepper.

Mix together rest of ingredients except paprika. Pour mixture over fish. Use generous amount of paprika on top. Cover. Bake at 325°F 45 to 60 minutes, until fish flakes when tested with a fork. Serve at once. Makes 4 to 6 servings.

baked fish fillets creole

1 pound fish fillets
2 tablespoons butter
½ medium onion, thinly sliced into rings
½ green pepper, thinly sliced
1 10½-ounce can condensed tomato soup
1 teaspoon vinegar
Dash of black pepper
Dash of hot pepper sauce (optional but nice)

Use well-greased shallow baking dish. Place fillets in single layer around dish.

Melt butter in saucepan; cook onion and green pepper until tender. Add soup, vinegar, pepper, and pepper sauce; stir until well-blended into tasty sauce. Pour over fish. Bake at 375°F 45 minutes or until fish is very tender.

Serve fillets over rice. Makes 4 servings.

fish fillets in creole sauce

1 medium onion, chopped
½ cup chopped celery
1 tablespoon butter
1 8-ounce can tomato sauce
½ teaspoon salt
½ teaspoon curry powder
Dash of freshly ground black pepper
2 pounds frozen fish fillets of your choice

Sauté onion and celery in butter in large skillet. Add rest of ingredients except fish. Simmer mixture while you cut fish blocks in thirds, giving you 6 pieces. Put fish in skillet, side by side. Do not pile them on each other. Bring to boil; reduce to simmer. Simmer about 15 minutes or until fish flakes easily to the fork. Makes 4 to 6 servings.

beer-batter fried shrimp

2 pounds shrimp, shelled, deveined
1 12-ounce can beer
1 cup flour
1 tablespoon salt
1 tablespoon paprika
Dash of red pepper to taste
Fat for deep frying

Shell and devein raw shrimp. Pour beer into large bowl. Blend dry ingredients into beer to make pancake-like batter. While using batter, stir from time to time. Thoroughly coat each shrimp with batter just before frying. Fry shrimp, a few at a time, in hot deep fat until golden brown and crusty. Drain cooked shrimp on paper towel; transfer to hot platter.

Serve shrimp piping hot. Makes about 6 servings.

shrimp gumbo

This gumbo is delicious served hot but also does well when chilled. It's just plain good anyway you serve it.

2 tablespoons oil
1 large eggplant, peeled, diced
3 green peppers, diced
¼ pound fresh okra, sliced in ½-inch rings
4 tomatoes, quartered
½ teaspoon sugar
Dash of cayenne pepper
1 pound shelled, deveined shrimp

Heat oil in large pot. Add all vegetables, sugar, and cayenne pepper. Cover; cook slowly 30 minutes, stirring several times. Uncover to allow stew to thicken; cook 30 minutes more. Add extra seasonings if needed, then throw in shrimp. Cook, covered, just 10 minutes more. Makes 6 servings.

seafood supreme

A fast put-together combined with delicious taste makes this dish truly supreme.

4 tablespoons chopped green pepper
2 tablespoons chopped green onion
1 cup chopped celery
1 cup crab meat
1 cup cooked shrimp
1 cup cold cooked rice
1 10-ounce package frozen peas
½ teaspoon salt
½ teaspoon Worcestershire sauce
½ teaspoon pepper
1 cup mayonnaise
Crushed potato chips for topping

Mix together ingredients, except topping, in large bowl. Put into greased casserole; cover with crushed potato chips. Bake at 325°F 30 minutes. Makes 4 to 6 servings.

tennessee fried fish

6 skinned, pan-dressed fish
2 teaspoons salt
¼ teaspoon pepper
2 eggs
2 tablespoons milk
2 cups cornmeal

Sprinkle fish on both sides with salt and pepper.

Beat eggs slightly; blend in milk.

Dip fish in eggs; roll in cornmeal. Place in heavy skillet containing about ⅛-inch melted fat, hot but not smoking. Fry at moderate heat. When fish is brown on one side, turn carefully; brown other side. Cooking time is about 10 minutes, depending on thickness of fish. Drain on paper towels.

Serve fish immediately on hot platter. Makes 6 servings.

crab-meat sauté

2 pounds fresh lump crab meat
1 cup tarragon vinegar
¼ pound plus 2 tablespoons butter
1 tablespoon chopped chives
1 tablespoon Worcestershire sauce
10 slices toast, cut into triangles

Pick over crab meat to remove any pieces of shell.

Heat vinegar, butter, chives, and Worcestershire sauce in deep heavy saucepan. Add crab meat, stirring gently until coated with sauce and quite hot.

Spoon crab meat over toast triangles; serve at once. Makes 8 to 10 servings.

tennessee fried fish

crab cakes

crab cakes

1 pound crab meat
1 egg yolk
1½ teaspoons salt
Healthy dash of black pepper
1 teaspoon dry mustard
2 teaspoons Worcestershire sauce
1 tablespoon mayonnaise
1 tablespoon chopped parsley
1 tablespoon melted butter
Bread crumbs for coating cakes
Liquid shortening for frying

Lightly toss crab meat and all ingredients (except bread crumbs) in order listed. When well-blended, shape into cakes. Roll each cake in bread crumbs until coated on all sides.

Heat shortening. Fry crab cakes quickly in hot fat until golden brown. Makes 4 to 6 servings.

soft-shelled crabs

This is a coastal delicacy where the crabs are obtainable when they have lost their hard shell. They are a seasonal favorite with most Southern people.

4 tablespoons butter
2 tablespoons lemon juice
6 to 8 soft-shelled crabs, cleaned
1 tablespoon cornstarch or flour
¼ cup water

Heat butter and lemon juice in medium-size skillet. Cook crabs on medium heat until browned, 5 minutes per side. Remove crabs to heated platter.

Mix cornstarch and water. Add to pan juices, stirring until slightly thickened. Pour sauce over crabs. Serve at once. Makes 4 to 6 servings.

oysters baltimore

These oysters are delicious served over hot buttered toast. Garnish with crumbled bacon.

4 slices bacon
18 oysters
3 tablespoons chili sauce
1 tablespoon Worcestershire sauce
6 tablespoons heavy cream
½ teaspoon tarragon
2 tablespoons lemon juice
1 teaspoon salt
¼ teaspoon pepper

Fry bacon until crisp. Set aside to drain; crumble into bits for garnish.

Pour off all but 1 tablespoon fat from skillet. Add oysters with their liquid. Cook, uncovered, over medium heat until most pan juices are absorbed.

Mix remaining ingredients. Add to oysters. Simmer no more than 5 minutes, to blend all flavors. Add extra seasonings if desired. Makes 4 to 6 servings.

crispy fish fry

This original recipe was for catfish, a favorite Southern food heritage. If you can't catch your own catfish, substitute any other fish, fresh or frozen. This is good eating.

6 skinned, pan-dressed fish
½ cup evaporated milk
1 tablespoon salt
Dash of freshly ground pepper
1 cup flour
½ cup yellow cornmeal
2 teaspoons paprika
12 slices bacon

Clean, wash, and dry fish.

Combine milk, salt, and pepper.

Combine flour, cornmeal, and paprika.

Dip fish in milk mixture; roll in flour mixture.

Fry bacon in heavy skillet until crisp. Remove bacon; reserve fat for frying. Drain bacon. Fry fish in hot fat 4 minutes. Turn carefully; fry 4 to 6 minutes longer or until fish is brown. Drain on paper towels.

Serve each fish portion with 2 bacon slices. Makes 6 servings.

vegetables

butter beans

Baby limas can be substituted for butter beans, if you prefer. Cook them the same way.

2 pounds small butter beans
½ cup water
2 tablespoons bacon drippings
1 teaspoon seasoned salt
1 onion, cut in half
½ teaspoon pepper
1 clove garlic (optional)
1 teaspoon salt
2 teaspoons cornstarch
1 tablespoon butter

Put all ingredients, except cornstarch and butter, into saucepan; cook until beans are tender, about 10 minutes. Remove onion and garlic; drain beans, reserving liquid.

Slightly thicken liquid with cornstarch. Add butter. Mix well; pour over beans. Serve at once. Makes 4 to 6 servings.

bean bundles

This is a variation of the Southern beans-and-bacon bits and makes an attractive bundle on the plate as well as good eating.

2 cans whole green beans
½ pound bacon

After beans are drained, divide them into bundles of 5 each. Wrap each bundle with ½ slice bacon; secure with toothpick. Broil on rack until bacon is cooked. Keep warm.

sauce
3 tablespoons butter
3 tablespoons tarragon vinegar
½ teaspoon salt
1 tablespoon chopped fresh parsley
1 tablespoon finely chopped onion

Place all ingredients in saucepan; simmer until hot.
Pour sauce over cooked bean bundles; serve. Makes 8 servings.

baked limas in cream

1 10-ounce package frozen lima beans
½ teaspoon Accent
½ teaspoon seasoned salt
Freshly ground pepper to taste
¾ cup milk or cream

Allow beans to thaw slightly so they can be put into greased 1-quart casserole. Sprinkle seasonings over beans. Pour milk on top. Cover casserole; bake at 350°F 20 minutes. Stir once. Reduce heat to 300°F; bake 20 minutes more. When beans are tender, dish is ready to be served. Makes 4 to 6 servings.

brussels sprouts

Although fresh brussels sprouts can be used for this recipe, they are not always available. In their absence, use frozen.

2 packages brussels sprouts
2 chicken bouillon cubes
½ cup sliced almonds
2 tablespoons butter
1 can cream of chicken soup
Dash of crushed thyme
1 small jar chopped pimientos
Dash of black pepper

Cook sprouts as directed on package, adding bouillon cubes to liquid. Drain.
Lightly sauté almonds in butter. Add soup; stir until well-blended. Add remaining seasonings to sauce.
Place brussels sprouts in casserole; cover with sauce. Heat in 350°F oven 20 minutes. Makes 6 servings.

hominy deluxe

This makes a winner because it looks and tastes so good.

½ pound pork sausage
3 cups canned hominy, drained
3 tablespoons chopped onion
1 cup canned tomato soup
½ teaspoon salt
½ cup seasoned bread or cracker crumbs

Cook sausage in medium-size skillet until fat begins to drain from it. Add hominy and onion; cook until all are browned and blended. Add tomato soup and salt; stir until hot.
Just before serving, top hominy with seasoned bread crumbs. Makes 4 to 6 servings.

fried okra

Fried okra may also be used as a good and healthy snack for hungry youngsters.

1 pound fresh young okra
½ to 1 cup cornmeal
Salt and pepper to taste
Fat for deep frying

Wash okra; cut into 1-inch pieces. Liberally sprinkle pieces with salt and pepper.
Put cornmeal into brown paper bag; shake seasoned okra in bag to coat each piece with meal. Fry in deep fat until golden brown and crisp. Drain on paper towel; keep warm until serving. Makes 4 to 6 servings.

okra plus

This is a delicious vegetable hot, but just as good when served cold.

3 slices bacon
1 cup sliced okra
1 large onion, finely chopped
1 cup chopped celery
6 tomatoes, chopped
1 green pepper, diced
1 hot red pepper, diced
Salt and pepper to taste
1 pint creamed corn

Fry bacon; when crisp, drain on paper towel.
Seal edges of okra in hot bacon fat. Add onion and celery; sauté until onion is transparent, not brown. Add tomatoes, peppers, salt, and pepper; cook 3 to 5 minutes. Add corn; simmer all together 20 minutes.
Just before serving, crumble bacon on top. Makes 6 to 8 servings.

carrot fritters

1 bunch carrots or 2 1-pound cans sliced carrots
1 egg
1 tablespoon sugar
3 tablespoons flour
Salt and pepper to taste
1 teaspoon baking powder
Deep fat for frying

If using raw carrots, cook them in small amount of water until very tender. Mash carrots fine; when pasty, add egg and sugar. Next add flour, salt, pepper, and baking powder; stir until well-blended. Drop by spoonfuls into deep fat. They will brown quickly when fat is right temperature. Drain fritters on paper towel; keep warm until all are finished. Serve at once. Makes 6 to 8 servings.

sweet pea special

Currant jelly is the hidden ingredient that makes these peas super. A party dish so easy to make you'll want it for the family, too.

5 tablespoons butter
3 tablespoons currant jelly
1 tablespoon sugar
2 cans small peas
Salt and freshly ground pepper to taste

Melt butter, currant jelly, and sugar in medium-size skillet. Heat peas in another saucepan. Drain off all but 1 cup liquid. Put peas and 1 cup liquid into jelly mixture. Season with salt and pepper. Simmer very gently until ready to serve. Makes 6 to 8 servings.

fried green tomatoes

This is an excellent way to use a bumper crop of tomatoes that has not ripened fast enough. Green tomatoes go well with corn on the cob—a true summer delight.

4 medium green tomatoes, sliced ½ inch thick
1 teaspoon salt
½ teaspoon pepper
1 teaspoon dillweed
1 cup cornmeal
Fat for frying

Wash and prepare tomatoes—and they must be green.

Mix seasonings with cornmeal in pie plate. Batter each tomato slice; be sure both sides are coated.

Heat fat in medium skillet. Cook tomatoes until brown on both sides. Drain on paper towels. Keep warm until ready to serve. Makes 4 to 6 servings.

41

skillet salad

1 large bowl fresh greens (collard, mustard, spinach, turnip, or beet)
6 to 8 bacon slices
1 tablespoon vinegar
1 cup seasoned croutons

Wash and dry greens. Chop or cut them into large salad bowl.

Fry bacon crisp in medium skillet; drain. Break slices into bits.

Add vinegar to fat left in skillet; stir until hot. Pour mixture over salad greens so that greens wilt. Add croutons; toss lightly. Salad is ready to eat. Makes 4 to 6 servings.

creamed celery with pecans

4 cups celery cut diagonally into ½-inch pieces
1 can cream of celery soup
1 teaspoon salt
¾ cup pecan halves
Buttered bread crumbs

Place celery in greased casserole. Add undiluted soup; sprinkle with salt. Sprinkle with pecans; cover all with buttered bread crumbs. Bake at 400°F 20 minutes. Makes 4 to 6 servings.

sweet-potato surprise

6 sweet potatoes
1 to 2 cups water
2 cups light-brown sugar
¼ pound butter
½ cup bourbon

Boil sweet potatoes in jackets until almost tender, about 15 minutes. Peel cooked potatoes; cut into large chunks.

Put layer of potatoes, 1 cup sugar, and 4 tablespoons butter in greased casserole. Repeat layers, dotting top with butter. Pour bourbon over all. Bake 40 minutes at 350°F. Serve at once. Makes 6 servings.

potato surprise

One surprise is that this is almost a meal in itself.
Another surprise is the delicious, delicate taste.

10 medium baking potatoes
½ pound butter
1 cup milk or cream (half-and-half will do)
1½ teaspoons salt
1½ teaspoons pepper
About 1 cup chopped green onions with tops
1 pound crab meat
1 cup grated Parmesan cheese

potato surprise

Bake potatoes at 450°F in your usual manner. Remove from oven;
cut lengthwise. Scoop out potato, leaving shell; mash with butter,
cream, salt, and pepper. Mix well. Add onions and crab meat, mixing gently but thoroughly. Fill potato shells with mixture. Top each
with grated cheese. Bake at 350°F 15 to 20 minutes or until cheese
has melted. Serve with pride. Makes 10 servings.

corn fritters

corn fritters

1 1-pound can whole-kernel corn, drained
1 egg
½ teaspoon salt
¼ cup milk
1 cup flour
2 teaspoons baking powder
2 teaspoons melted butter
½ teaspoon sugar
Deep fat for frying

While corn is draining, mix egg, salt, milk, flour, baking powder,
melted butter, and sugar. Stir with long-handled wooden spoon.
Add drained corn. Allow mixture to sit 5 minutes. Drop by teaspoonfuls into hot fat. Cook until puffy and golden brown. Drain
on paper; transfer to warmed platter. Makes 4 to 6 servings.

salads

fresh banana salad

6 medium bananas
Lemon juice
Salad greens (Try spinach!)
½ cup mayonnaise
½ cup smooth peanut butter

Slice bananas; sprinkle with lemon juice. Arrange on individual plates of salad greens.

Blend mayonnaise and peanut butter; pour over salad. Serve at once. Makes 4 to 6 servings.

easy bing-cherry mold

1 1-pound can bing cherries, pitted
1 6-ounce package lemon gelatin
2¾ cups hot water
½ cup chopped nuts

Drain cherries; reserve 1 cup juice.

Dissolve gelatin in hot water; add reserved cherry juice. Allow mixture to set slightly 1 hour in refrigerator. Add cherries and nuts; pour into ring mold. Refrigerate several hours or overnight. Turn out mold onto bed of crisp greens. Makes 4 to 6 servings.

red-raspberry salad

This salad makes any meal a party.

2 cans frozen red raspberries, drained
1 16-ounce can crushed pineapple, drained
1 12-ounce can frozen orange juice, thawed, undiluted
2 packages (3-ounce size) red-raspberry gelatin
1 cup boiling water

Thaw and drain raspberries; reserve juice.

Drain pineapple; reserve juice. Add orange juice to drained juices so that liquid measures 2½ cups.

Dissolve gelatin in boiling water. Add juices; chill until partially set. Add raspberries and pineapple. Pour into greased 2-quart mold; chill until set. Makes 10 to 12 servings.

carrot salad

1 small onion, finely chopped
1 medium pepper, finely chopped
3 ribs celery, finely chopped
2 1-pound cans sliced carrots, drained
1 cup tomato soup, undiluted
1 cup sugar
¼ cup oil
¾ cup cider vinegar
1 tablespoon dry mustard
1 tablespoon Worcestershire sauce
Lettuce leaves, washed, drained

Add onion, pepper, and celery to drained carrots; set aside.

Put soup, sugar, oil, vinegar, mustard, and Worcestershire sauce into small saucepan. Bring to boil, so that all ingredients blend. Pour over vegetables. When cool, refrigerate to chill thoroughly, at least overnight.

Serve salad on crisp lettuce leaves. Makes 10 to 12 servings.

hominy salad

This adaptable recipe can be varied with any number of cooked, diced vegetables as they are available from the garden. Be creative with this—add; change. Vary and enjoy.

2 bacon strips, cut into bits
2 cups cooked hominy
1 large onion, diced
1 teaspoon salt
¼ cup vinegar
½ teaspoon sugar

Cook bacon bits slowly over low heat. When bacon is crisp, pour bacon and pan-fat over hominy.

Return skillet to low heat; add onion, salt, vinegar, and sugar. Bring mixture to boil; pour over hominy and bacon. Toss gently; add extra seasonings if needed.

This salad can be served as is or slightly chilled. Makes 4 to 6 servings.

overnight crab salad

overnight crab salad

This salad improves if made the night before. It must be refrigerated at least 4 hours. It goes together in a jiffy and is sure to bring compliments to the cook.

2 cups crab meat
1 large onion, finely chopped
1 tablespoon chopped parsley
1 teaspoon Accent
Dash of Tabasco sauce
1 tablespoon Worcestershire sauce
Salt and pepper to taste
½ cup oil
½ cup vinegar
Avocado or tomato slices or lettuce

Put crab meat in bowl; cover with chopped onion. Add seasonings to oil and vinegar; pour over crab and onions. Toss lightly to mix all flavors. Cover; refrigerate overnight.

Serve salad on sliced avocado or tomato or lettuce. Makes 4 to 6 servings.

tomato-soup salad dressing

¼ cup sugar
½ cup vinegar
1 cup oil
1 can tomato soup, undiluted
Salt and pepper to taste

Mix ingredients together in bowl, using whisk or egg-beater. When thoroughly blended, put in glass bottle; store in refrigerator until ready to use. Makes about 3 cups.

dandelion salad

Feel virtuous if you have taken the dandelion greens from your own yard—called weeding and feeding at the same time!

½ **pound tender, young dandelion greens**
½ **cup thinly sliced red or Spanish onions**
2 tomatoes, cut in fourths
Cut-up or shredded cheese
Salt and pepper to taste
Your favorite French dressing or oil and vinegar

Wash dandelion greens; drain well. Cut into 2-inch pieces. Add rest of ingredients in order given; toss to mix well. Makes 4 servings.

black-eyed peas supreme

2 1-pound cans black-eyed peas, drained
1 onion, sliced into thin rings
½ **cup olive oil**
¼ **cup wine vinegar**
1 medium clove garlic, mashed
1 tablespoon Worcestershire sauce
1 teaspoon salt
Pepper to taste

Place peas and onion in ovenproof bowl.
Combine olive oil, vinegar, and seasonings in small pan. Bring to boil; pour immediately over peas and onions. Stir gently. Refrigerate salad several hours or overnight.
When thoroughly chilled, the flavors will all blend together. Eat and enjoy. Makes 8 servings.

sassy sauerkraut salad

1 1-pound can sauerkraut
1 cup chopped green pepper
1 cup chopped onion
1 small can chopped pimientos (optional)
1 cup sugar
1 cup white vinegar

Drain sauerkraut thoroughly. Add chopped vegetables; mix well.
Bring sugar and vinegar to boil, but do not boil. This will thoroughly dissolve sugar. Pour over slaw mixture; toss thoroughly. Chill in covered bowl in refrigerator at least several hours. Overnight is even better. This dish will keep well several days. Makes about 6 servings.

spinach–orange– avocado salad

3 cups fresh spinach, trimmed, washed
2 11-ounce cans mandarin oranges, drained
1 cup diced avocado
¼ **cup French dressing**

Tear spinach into small pieces. Combine with other ingredients; toss lightly. Chill, but serve within an hour or 2 of the toss. The subtle blend of flavors gets lost if the spinach is too wilted. Makes 4 to 6 servings.

hot slaw

When you're looking for one hot dish to go with a cold dinner, this is it. Easy, tangy, and different.

2 tablespoons salad oil	½ teaspoon celery seeds
4 cups shredded cabbage	¼ teaspoon pepper
½ teaspoon salt	2 tablespoons vinegar

Heat salad oil in medium-size skillet. Add cabbage and seasonings, but not vinegar. Cover; cook over medium heat about 3 minutes. Be sure to stir occasionally to mix flavors. Last, add vinegar; stir again.

Serve slaw at once and hot. Makes 4 to 6 servings.

tomato aspic

1 3-ounce package lemon gelatin	1 cup finely diced celery
½ cup hot water	1 cup chopped nuts
1 can tomato soup, undiluted	

Dissolve gelatin in hot water; stir until it is liquid. Add soup; stir to blend. Put in celery and nuts. Pour into individual molds; chill until set, at least 2 hours.

Unmold aspic; serve on crisp lettuce leaves. Makes 4 servings.

corn-stuffed tomato salad

6 medium tomatoes	¼ cup vegetable oil
1½ cups whole-kernel corn, drained	1 tablespoon lemon juice
¼ cup chopped green onions	1 small garlic clove, minced
⅓ cup chopped green pepper	Lettuce or salad greens
½ teaspoon salt	

Spoon out centers of tomatoes; chill. Mix centers with corn, onions, green pepper, and salt. Chill tomato cups during mixing process.

Combine vegetable oil, lemon juice, and garlic. Pour over mixed vegetables; chill.

When ready to serve, spoon vegetables into tomato cups. Place on salad greens and feel extra virtuous—only 150 calories per tomato. Makes 6 servings.

buttermilk salad dressing

This is a low-calorie salad dressing that can be made ahead and stored in the refrigerator. When spooned out, each tablespoon is only 6 calories.

1 pint buttermilk	1 clove garlic, finely crushed
Juice of 1 lemon	Salt and pepper to taste

Place all ingredients in jar with tight-fitting lid. Shake well to mix; refrigerator at least overnight. Shake well just before using. Makes 1 pint.

tomato and onion salad

Peanut oil is what Southern cooks use for this marinade, but you may substitute your regular salad oil if you insist. If you do substitute, grate some peanuts into the marinade for flavor.

¼ cup peanut oil
1 tablespoon chopped parsley
1 teaspoon salt
¼ teaspoon pepper
3 medium tomatoes, cut in wedges
3 medium onions, sliced in thin rings
Lettuce leaves

Combine peanut oil and seasonings; stir well. Pour over tomatoes and onions; marinate at least 30 minutes.

When ready, spoon salad onto crisp lettuce leaves; serve. Makes 4 to 6 servings.

salamagundy

You might think this is just a chef's salad when you put it together, but call it Salamagundy. Then tell your guests it was served in eighteenth-century England and brought to this country by our forefathers.

1 head lettuce
1 head romaine
1 cup sliced ham, cut into strips
1 cup sliced chicken, cut into strips
4 hard-cooked eggs, sliced
1 can anchovies
8 to 10 sweet pickles, sliced
Your favorite oil and vinegar dressing

Wash and drain lettuce and romaine; arrange on 8 salad plates. Spread remaining ingredients over tops of greens. Pour salad dressing over all; serve chilled. Makes 8 servings.

zero salad dressing

This is a delicious low-calorie dressing that is nice to have around the house for a fast salad. Since most of the ingredients are staples in the kitchen, you can always whip this up in a hurry.

½ cup tomato juice
2 tablespoons lemon juice or vinegar
1 tablespoon finely chopped onion
Salt and pepper to taste

Place all ingredients in jar with tight-fitting lid. Shake well each time before using.

This flavor can be varied by adding chopped parsley, dill, green pepper, horseradish, or mustard—as the whim takes you. Makes dressing for 1 salad.

breads

batter bread

Serve this good bread with plenty of butter. It will be eaten very fast.

1 cup milk
3 tablespoons sugar
2 teaspoons salt
1½ tablespoons butter
1 cup warm water
2 packages dry yeast
4½ cups flour

Heat the milk, sugar, salt, and butter on low heat until butter has melted and sugar and salt dissolved. Do not boil. Set aside to cool slightly.

Add yeast to warm water; stir until dissolved. Add cooled mixture. Gradually add in flour; stir until all is well-blended. Cover with towel; store in warm place to rise about 40 minutes.

Stir down batter; beat a few vigorous strokes. Divide into 2 parts; place each in well-greased round casserole. Bake at 375°F ½ hour to 45 minutes, until nicely crusted on top. Cool on rack. Makes 2 round loaves.

bacon bread

2 cups flour
1 teaspoon salt
3 teaspoons baking powder
⅔ cup sugar
¾ cup smooth peanut butter

1 egg, beaten
1 cup milk
¼ cup bacon drippings
½ cup crumbled crisp bacon

Combine all ingredients in order given, blending thoroughly. Be sure bacon is distributed all through batter. Pour batter into well-greased 9 × 5 × 2-inch loaf pan; set aside at least 15 minutes. Bake at 350°F 50 to 55 minutes. Turn out on rack to cool. Slice bread; serve. Makes 1 loaf.

dilly bread

dilly bread

1 package dry yeast
¼ cup warm water
1 cup cottage cheese,
   room temperature
2 tablespoons sugar
1 tablespoon instant onion

1 tablespoon butter
2 teaspoons dillseed
1 teaspoon salt
¼ teaspoon soda
1 unbeaten egg
2¼ cups flour

Soften yeast in warm water. Add lukewarm cottage cheese, sugar, onion, butter, dillseed, salt, soda, and egg. Stir well. Add flour to form stiff dough. Finish kneading bread with your hands. When dough is well-kneaded, cover; let rise in warm place at least 60 minutes.

Beat down batter; place in greased 1½-quart round casserole. Allow to rise 40 minutes more.

Bake at 350°F 45 minutes. Turn out bread onto rack. While still hot, brush top with melted butter and sprinkle with salt. Makes 1 loaf.

skillet bread

This is simple to mix, tricky to turn in the skillet, and so good dripping with melted butter and jelly.

2 cups flour
4 teaspoons baking powder
2 teaspoons salt

1¼ cups milk
2 tablespoons butter

Mix dry ingredients in bowl. Add milk; blend with wooden spoon. Will have biscuit-like spongy texture.

Heat butter in medium-size skillet. Keep heat low. Spread butter around evenly. Pour in batter. Cook 15 minutes or until underside is golden brown. Here's the tricky part. Lift with large spatula; turn to cook other side 15 minutes.

Turn bread out onto round plate; serve at once. Makes 1 loaf, 4 to 6 servings.

corn bread

1 cup flour
¾ cup cornmeal (yellow preferred)
1 teaspoon salt
1 tablespoon baking powder
4 tablespoons sugar
1 cup milk
2 eggs
4 tablespoons melted butter

Place dry ingredients in bowl.

Combine milk, egg, and butter in 2-cup measure, beating well with a fork.

Make well in dry ingredients; pour in liquids. Blend gently; do not overbeat. Pour batter into 8-inch-square greased pan. Bake at 400°F 30 minutes. Corn bread is done when you can stick it with a toothpick and the toothpick comes out clean.

Cut bread into squares; serve. Makes 12 to 16 pieces.

sweet-potato biscuits

When a son-in-law remembers his grandmother's sweet-potato biscuits dripping with butter and jam, that's a recipe to be included with love. So here it is.

¾ cup mashed sweet potatoes
⅔ cup milk
4 tablespoons melted butter
1¼ cups flour
4 teaspoons baking powder
1 tablespoon sugar
½ teaspoon salt

Combine well-mashed sweet potatoes with milk and melted butter. Add dry ingredients in order given to form soft dough. Drop moist dough into well-greased muffin pans. Bake in hot (450°F) oven about 15 minutes.

Dough can be turned out onto floured board, tossed until smooth on outside, then rolled out ½ inch thick and cut with biscuit cutter. Place cut biscuits on greased pan; bake as above. Makes about 24 biscuits.

pecan whole-wheat muffins

1 cup all-purpose flour
3 teaspoons baking powder
4 tablespoons sugar
1 teaspoon salt
1 cup whole-wheat flour

1 cup chopped pecans
4 tablespoons melted butter
1 cup milk
2 eggs

Mix all-purpose flour, baking powder, sugar, and salt together in medium-size bowl. Add and stir in whole-wheat flour and nuts. Add butter, milk, and eggs to dry ingredients; blend until thoroughly moistened. Spoon batter into well-greased muffin tins. Bake at 375°F 15 to 18 minutes. Makes 12 muffins.

popovers

2 eggs
1 cup milk
1 cup flour
½ teaspoon salt
1 tablespoon melted butter

Use a wooden spoon to mix together all ingredients in order given. Fill 6 to 8 well-greased custard cups (you may prefer to use muffin tins) half full. Bake at 475°F for 30 minutes, then lower oven to 350°F for 30 minutes. Just before you take popovers from oven, prick each with fork to allow air to escape.

Serve popovers at once, piping hot, with plenty of butter. Makes 6 to 8.

pecan waffles

1½ cups flour
1½ tablespoons sugar
2½ teaspoons baking powder
½ teaspoon salt
3 eggs, separated, whites beaten stiff
1½ cups milk
5 tablespoons melted butter
¼ cup chopped pecans

Measure dry ingredients into 4-cup measure; set aside.

Beat egg yolks until thick; combine with milk and butter. Add dry ingredients. When batter is well-mixed, gently add pecans. Fold in egg whites. Bake in hot waffle iron.

Serve waffles with your favorite syrup or cinnamon mixed with sugar. Makes 5 to 6 servings.

pecan waffles

orange bread

orange bread

3 cups flour
3 tablespoons baking powder
⅔ cup sugar
1 teaspoon salt

1¼ cups milk
2 tablespoons melted butter
1 egg, beaten
Peel of 1 orange, finely chopped

Measure dry ingredients into 4-cup measure. Sift them into mixing bowl. Add milk, butter, and egg; mix with wooden spoon. Add orange peel. (If you prefer, you can substitute 1 to 2 tablespoons prepared orange bits.) Place mixture in greased loaf pan, 9 × 5 × 2 inches. Let rise 15 minutes.

Bake bread in moderate (350°F) oven 50 minutes. Makes 1 loaf.

sally lunn bread

This hot bread is named after the English lady who sold it on the streets of England in the eighteenth century. It became a favorite in the American colonies and still is today.

1 cup milk
¼ pound butter
¼ cup water
4 cups flour

⅓ cup sugar
2 teaspoons salt
2 packages dry yeast
3 eggs

Heat milk, butter, and water until warm enough to melt butter, but not boiling. Set aside. Place 1⅓ cups flour, sugar, salt, and yeast in large bowl. Add warm liquids to this mixture. Beat with electric mixer 2 minutes to blend. Gradually add ⅔ cup more flour and eggs. Beat at high speed 2 minutes. Scrape sides of bowl with rubber spatula. Add remaining flour; mix well until batter is thick but not stiff. Cover; let rise 1½ hours.

Beat dough down with spatula; turn out into well-greased 10-inch tube pan or bundt pan. Cover; let rise in warm place about 30 to 45 minutes.

Bake at 350°F 40 to 50 minutes. To release Sally Lunn from pan, run knife around outer edges; turn onto plate to cool, but not too much. Sally Lunn is delicious served warm. Makes 1 large loaf.

corn muffins

This is a good recipe to double. Make 1 dozen to serve at once and 12 to freeze for another meal.

1 cup cornmeal
1 cup flour
1 teaspoon salt
2½ teaspoons baking powder
1 cup milk
2 eggs, beaten well
2 tablespoons shortening, melted

Place dry ingredients in large mixing bowl.

Combine milk and eggs in smaller bowl; add to dry ingredients. Stir in shortening until all ingredients are well-blended. Drop by spoonfuls into 2-inch greased muffin tins, filling tins about half full. Bake at 400°F about 20 minutes.

Serve muffins with hot butter and your favorite jam or jelly, or break muffins in half, cover with syrup, and eat with a fork. They're delicious any way you prefer. Makes 12 muffins.

hush puppies

½ cup flour
2 teaspoons baking powder
½ teaspoon salt
1½ cups cornmeal
1 small onion, finely chopped
¾ cup milk
1 egg, beaten
Deep fat for frying

Put dry ingredients into large bowl in order listed. Add onion, then milk and egg. Stir until all ingredients are well-blended.

Heat fat in deep skillet. Drop batter by teaspoonfuls into hot fat; fry until golden brown all over. Remove; drain hush puppies on paper towels. Keep warm until ready to serve.

To vary hush puppies, use above recipe, substituting ½ cup chopped apple or ½ cup cooked corn in place of onion. Makes about 2 dozen.

buttermilk hush puppies

2 cups cornmeal
1 tablespoon flour
1 teaspoon baking powder
1 teaspoon salt
½ teaspoon baking soda
1 cup buttermilk
1 egg, beaten
Deep fat for frying

Place dry ingredients in bowl. Add buttermilk and egg; mix well until it is a smooth batter. Drop batter by spoonfuls into hot fat; fry until crispy brown all over. Drain on paper towels; serve at once. Makes about 2 dozen.

desserts

lemon ice-cream pie

1 half-gallon vanilla ice cream
1 6-ounce can frozen lemonade
2 8-inch graham-cracker crusts
Graham-cracker crumbs for garnish

Melt ice cream and lemonade; beat together until a creamy texture. Pour into graham-cracker crusts; place in freezer until serving time. (This can be several hours later or several days later.)

When ready to serve, sprinkle each pie with graham-cracker crumbs for garnish. Makes 8 to 10 servings.

ambrosia

There are as many variations of this dessert as there are cooks. Use your own ideas to add your touch to ambrosia—food truly fit for the gods.

3 fresh oranges, peeled, sectioned
3 fresh grapefruits, peeled, sectioned
½ fresh pineapple, peeled, diced
⅓ cup orange juice

¼ cup light corn syrup
½ cup shredded flaked or fresh coconut

Prepare fruit as indicated above.

Combine orange juice and syrup; pour over fruit. Stir in coconut; reserve some for garnish. Spoon mixture into 6 sherbet glasses; sprinkle coconut on top of each glass. Chill until ready to serve. Makes 6 servings.

P.S. If you like the flavor of dry sherry or bourbon, add ¼ cup to the liquids and allow fruit to ripen in this mixture.

fresh apple cookies

Don't let this long list of ingredients stop you. These cookies go together easily and are well worth the time. They taste delicious.

¼ pound butter
1½ cups firmly packed
   brown sugar
½ teaspoon salt
½ teaspoon nutmeg
1 teaspoon cloves
1 teaspoon cinnamon
1 egg

2 cups flour
1 teaspoon baking soda
1 cup finely chopped
   unpeeled apples
1 cup raisins
1 cup chopped pecans
¼ cup milk

Blend first 7 ingredients with electric beater until smooth. Add flour and soda. Stir in apples, raisins, pecans, and milk; blend well. Drop from teaspoon onto greased cookie sheet, allowing room for batter to spread. Bake at 400°F 12 to 15 minutes. If you want to store any, do so in a tin; use waxed paper between each layer to avoid cookies sticking to each other. Makes about 6 dozen.

cinnamon squares

½ pound butter
1 cup sugar
1 egg, separated
2 cups flour
1½ tablespoons cinnamon
1 teaspoon salt
1½ cups chopped nuts

Cream butter and sugar; add egg yolk. Add flour, cinnamon, and salt. Press batter into generously greased 8 × 14-inch pan or 2 8-inch-square pans.

Beat egg white until foamy. Spread on top of batter. (You will not need all the egg white for this.) Press chopped nuts on top. Bake at 325°F 30 minutes. Allow to cool slightly; cut into squares. Makes about 48 squares.

peanut-butter cookies

These cookies can be made ahead and stored.

4 tablespoons butter
½ cup brown sugar
½ cup white sugar
1 egg
1 cup peanut butter
½ teaspoon salt
½ teaspoon baking soda
1½ cups flour

Cream butter and both sugars together. Add egg and peanut butter. When thoroughly creamed, add blended dry ingredients; mix until all flour is absorbed. Roll dough into balls about 1 inch in diameter; place on greased cookie sheet. Press each ball with fork dipped in cold water to flatten. Bake at 375°F 15 minutes. Makes about 24 cookies.

scotch shortbread

Traditionally, this shortbread is made in small pie-shaped wedges. If you prefer a pattern of squares, use 2 8-inch-square pans instead of pie pans. Either way, do not cut the finished shortbread with a knife. Break it along the lines you have pricked with a fork before baking. These are crumbly cookies but are delicious for dessert or a light fare with tea.

1 pound butter, room temperature
6 cups flour
1½ cups sugar
½ cup cornstarch

Place ingredients in order given in large mixing bowl. You may want to start cutting butter into dry ingredients with knives, but the best way is to use your hands to mix up the dough. When nothing sticks to sides of bowl, pat out dough ½ inch thick in pie pans or square pans. Prick dough to make size pieces you prefer. Bake at 350°F about 20 minutes or until edges start to brown. Remove from pan; break on pricked lines. Makes 30 to 40 pieces.

snickerdoodles

All the variations of this particular Southern cookie are good and this one is easy, too.

¼ pound butter
¾ cup sugar
1 egg
2 cups flour
1½ teaspoons baking powder
½ teaspoon salt
½ cup milk
½ teaspoon vanilla
2 tablespoons sugar mixed with 2 teaspoons cinnamon

Use wooden mixing spoon or electric beater to cream butter and sugar. Add egg. Alternate adding dry ingredients and milk, starting and ending with flour. Add vanilla. Stir until well-blended. Drop by teaspoons onto cookie sheet. Sprinkle each mound with sugar and cinnamon mixture. Bake at 400°F 15 minutes or until edges are slightly browned. Makes 50 to 60 cookies.

rice pudding deluxe

So good-tasting and so easy, too.

2 cups cooked rice
½ teaspoon salt
1 20-ounce can crushed pineapple, drained
½ pint whipped cream, beaten stiff

Mix rice, salt, and pineapple until well-blended. Add most of whipped cream; reserve some for garnish. Fold in gently.
Spoon pudding into individual serving dishes; top with whipped cream. Makes 6 to 8 servings.

fruit cobbler

¼ pound butter, melted
1 cup sugar
1 cup flour
1 teaspoon baking powder

1 cup milk
1 cup drained fruit, fresh
  or canned

Pour melted butter into 1½-quart Pyrex oven dish. Stir in sugar, flour, and baking powder; mix well. Slowly stir in milk. Last, fold in fruit. (This is a gentle process and should be done with a wooden spoon.) Bake at 350°F 1 hour.

This may be served hot or warm and is good topped with either ice cream or whipped cream. Makes 6 servings.

linda's carrot cake

1½ cups flour
1½ cups sugar
1 teaspoon baking powder
1 teaspoon salt
½ teaspoon baking soda
½ teaspoon cinnamon
½ teaspoon nutmeg

½ teaspoon ginger
¾ cup cooking oil
3 eggs
3 teaspoons hot water
1 cup cooked mashed carrots
  (canned will do)
½ cup walnuts

Mix dry ingredients together in order given. Add cooking oil, eggs, water, and carrots; stir until well-blended. Add walnuts. Pour batter into ungreased cake or tube pan. Bake at 350°F 45 minutes. Makes 8 to 10 servings.

linda's carrot cake

orange nut bars

3 eggs
6 ounces frozen orange-juice
  concentrate
1 cup sugar
2 cups graham-cracker crumbs

¼ teaspoon salt
1 cup chopped nuts
8 ounces pitted dates, chopped
1 teaspoon vanilla

Beat eggs with orange-juice concentrate until light. Stir in remaining ingredients in order given. Spoon mixture into greased 8- or 9-inch-square pan. Bake at 350°F 50 minutes. Remove from oven; cool in pan on rack. Frost with Orange Icing; cut into bars. Makes 21 to 28 bars.

orange icing
1¼ cups confectioners' sugar
2½ tablespoons orange juice

Mix sugar and orange juice together until smooth and spreadable.

pecan crisp cookies

2½ cups flour
½ teaspoon salt
½ teaspoon baking soda
½ pound butter
1 pound light brown sugar

2 eggs, well-beaten
1 teaspoon vanilla
1 cup finely chopped pecans
Pecan halves for garnish

Measure flour, salt, and soda; set aside. Thoroughly cream butter; gradually add brown sugar until well-creamed together. Add eggs. Next add dry ingredients. Add vanilla; stir in chopped pecans. Drop by teaspoon onto cookie sheet, about 2 inches apart. Top with pecan halves if desired. Bake at 350°F about 10 minutes. Store in a tin or tightly closed container. Makes 5 to 6 dozen.

pecan fudge squares

This old family recipe crops up in many families and is always a popular one. Cut small, the squares can be bite-size delicacies fit for a party tray, and in larger squares each makes about two good bites.

1 pound brown sugar
½ pound butter
2 eggs, well-beaten
1½ cups flour

2 teaspoons baking powder
1 cup chopped pecans
1 teaspoon vanilla

Dissolve brown sugar in melted butter; allow to cool slightly. Add eggs, flour, and baking powder. Add nuts and vanilla; mix well. Pour into well-greased 9 × 14-inch pan. Bake at 350°F 20 to 30 minutes. Allow to cool slightly before cutting.

These squares can be frozen in 1 long piece or 2 large squares and cut into desired sizes when ready to serve. Makes about 48 squares.

pecan fudge squares

pound cake

½ pound butter
2 cups sugar
4 eggs, separated
3 cups flour
3 teaspoons baking powder

1 cup milk
1 teaspoon vanilla
¼ teaspoon nutmeg
(Be generous!)

Cream butter and sugar with electric beater. Add egg yolks 1 at a time.

Beat egg whites until very stiff; set aside.

Combine flour and baking powder. Add some of flour mixture and some of milk to creamed mixture; repeat until all milk has been used. Add vanilla and nutmeg. Fold in egg whites with rubber spatula, gently but firmly. Pour into 2 greased 9 × 5-inch loaf pans. Bake at 350°F 45 minutes or until testing toothpick comes out dry. Makes 2 loaves.

pound cake

bourbon balls

2 cups finely rolled vanilla wafers
2 tablespoons cocoa
1½ cups confectioners' sugar

1 cup finely chopped pecans
2 tablespoons white corn syrup
¼ cup bourbon

Mix wafer crumbs, cocoa, and 1 cup confectioners' sugar. Add chopped pecans. Stir in corn syrup and bourbon; mix well. Dust hands with a little powdered sugar; roll mixture into 1-inch balls. Roll each ball in remaining confectioners' sugar until well-coated.

Bourbon balls can be stored between layers of waxed paper in refrigerator or in sealed metal container at least 12 hours before serving. They store well several weeks in closed tin.

If you prefer flavor of rum or brandy, substitute ¼ cup of your preference for bourbon. Makes 36 to 42 balls.

sweet-potato pudding

2 cups peeled and grated
  sweet potatoes
1 cup sugar
1 tablespoon flour
¼ pound butter, melted

2 cups milk
½ teaspoon salt
1 teaspoon nutmeg
½ teaspoon cinnamon

Grate potatoes into large bowl. Stir in rest of ingredients in order given. Mixture will be fairly liquid. Pour into buttered baking dish. Bake at 350°F 2 hours.

This pudding tastes best if served slightly warm. Makes 6 to 8 servings.

sweet georgia peach pie

sweet georgia peach pie

1 unbaked pie shell
6 to 8 large fresh peaches, peeled, sliced
4 eggs, well-beaten
1 cup sugar
2 tablespoons flour
2 tablespoons melted shortening

Prepare pie shell; fill with sliced peaches.

Beat eggs well in bowl; add sugar, flour, and shortening. Pour over peaches. It will form its own top crust in baking. Bake at 400°F 15 minutes. Lower oven to 325°F; cook 40 minutes more. Allow to cool to room temperature. Slice, serve, and enjoy. Makes 1 9-inch pie.

pecan pie

To serve a large family, this favorite of the South should be made in an 11-inch pie pan and topped with rich whipped cream. You can use this recipe to make a fuller pie in a 9-inch pan if you prefer.

1 unbaked pie shell
5 eggs
¾ cup sugar
1½ cups dark Karo syrup
1½ cups pecans, chopped
  or halved

¾ teaspoon salt
2 teaspoons vanilla
Whipped cream for decoration

Prepare pie shell; set aside.

Beat eggs slightly in large bowl. Add sugar, syrup, nuts, salt, and vanilla; mix until nicely blended. Pour into pie shell. Bake at 325°F 50 minutes.

When cool, garnish pie with whipped cream; serve at once. Makes 6 to 8 servings.

spicy sweet-potato pie

This pie goes together in a hurry, and the result is a gourmet's delight. The house smells good while the pie is baking, and the taste is special.

1½ cups cooked, mashed
  sweet potatoes
½ cup sugar
1 teaspoon cinnamon
1 teaspoon allspice

½ teaspoon salt
3 eggs, well-beaten
1 cup milk
2 tablespoons butter, melted
1 9-inch unbaked pie shell

Mash sweet potatoes into fine paste. Add sugar, cinnamon, allspice, and salt. Add eggs to mixture.

Mix milk and melted butter together; stir into potato mixture. Mixture will be fairly liquid. Pour into unbaked pastry shell. Bake at 350°F 40 to 45 minutes. Makes 6 to 8 servings.

Index